Anarchy

ALSO BY MARK SCROGGINS

Bodhrán Songs/Eight Poems (with E. A. Miller) (1991)

Upper Limit Music:
The Writing of Louis Zukofsky (editor) (1997)

Louis Zukofsky and the Poetry of Knowledge (1998)

"Additional Prose," in Prepositions+:
The Collected Critical Essays of
Louis Zukofsky (editor) (2000)

Anarchy

Mark Scroggins

© 2003 Mark Scroggins
ISBN 1-881471-74-8

LCCN: 2002114152

Spuyten Duyvil
PO Box 1852
Cathedral Station
NYC 10025
1-800-886-5304
http://spuytenduyvil.net

Acknowledgments

Some of these poems were previously published in the journals *Green Zero, TO, Talisman, Facture, LSR, FlashPoint, Elixir,* and *Ur-Vox,* and in the anthology *The Gertrude Stein Awards in Innovative Poetry, 1994-1995* (Sun & Moon Press). My thanks to all of the editors. Others of them appeared in a limited edition chapbook, *Bodhrán Songs/Eight Poems* (with E. A. Miller) in 1991.

Contents

Bodhrán Song..........11
Springing..........12
Brownstone, Rubber Hose..........14
The Encroachment of History in October 1993..........16
Charles his ear *(Anarchy for the U.K.)*..........18
Milton's empty *(Anarchy for the U.K.)*..........20
Covnant *(Anarchy for the U.K.)*..........22
Liveforever Dayglow..........23
Swimming..........24
Broken Book..........25
struggle *(Anarchy for the U.K.)*..........28
Cromwell's achievements *(Anarchy for the U.K.)*..........30
Basilikon Doron *(Anarchy for the U.K.)*..........31
Eleven-Odd Propositions..........32
The Effacement of Genitalia..........33
Florida Poem 2..........36
Pipe Bands in Alexandria..........39
wee song..........41
Couenant of Peace *(Anarchy for the U.K.)*..........50
Circumstances considered *(Anarchy for the U.K.)*..........52
her proper voice *(Anarchy for the U.K.)*..........54
Video Memories..........56
the factory..........57
writing Ruskin..........58
The Passing of Eeyore..........60
the holy bede *(Anarchy for the U.K.)*..........62
tourist *(Anarchy for the U.K.)*..........65
fire & brimstone *(Pillars of Lot's Wife)* *(Anarchy for the U.K.)*..........68
Mark you *(Anarchy for the U.K.)*..........71
Albatross *(Anarchy for the U.K.)*..........73
Rote Song/Valentine..........75

for Jenny

> ...the Throne
> of *Chaos*, and his dark Pavilion spread
> Wide on the wasteful Deep; with him Enthron'd
> Sat Sable-vested *Night*, eldest of things,
> The Consort of his Reign; and by them stood
> *Orcus* and *Ades*, and the dreaded name
> Of *Demogorgon*; *Rumor* next and *Chance*,
> And *Tumult* and *Confusion* all imbroild,
> And *Discord* with a thousand various mouths.
>
> —*Paradise Lost* II.959-967

You can't place one record above the other, not while you're listening; each one is the end of the world, the creation of the world, complete in itself. Every good punk record made in London in 1976 or 1977 can convince you that it's the greatest thing you've ever heard because it can convince you that you never have to hear anything else as long as you live—each record seems to say everything there is to say. For as long as the sound lasts, no other sound, not even a memory of any other music, can penetrate.

—Greil Marcus, *Lipstick Traces: A Secret History of the Twentieth Century*

Bodhrán Song

daylong rearticulation
        shadow on the
blind

mute. round. oracular turning
reel in the flick'ring light
        all 'round the packing cases

patterned shifting, &
        melody   the hand losing
its fire the eye   its cunning

        nightshade : dayshade
        gloaming : dawn
        nightshower : dayburst

stepped-dance *slipjig* tracer
dust in the opaque streaming
        thru sound-hole's bridge

light-trickle Cross moted plectrum
        still "piping of plenty"
beauty: too lost place on the drum

Springing

That it was a perfect day, fitted together fiercely
and hardly in its particulars, could scarcely
be denied; you took that sun to heart, moved
and chastened by the clarity of the branches between.

I rolled my troubles into an old kit bag, caught
at the last vacillations of the ancient moon, drew carefully
the lines beyond which we had no connaisance, and
felt—"in my heart"—a motion which again refused denial.

What more could they do? They stood in the gloom
before the screen, which slowly scrolled its credits over
their clothes and faces. The rustling of the early
frost transfused a breathy, whispered singing, echoed

through the lobby and the darkened restrooms. The pants,
the socks, the underwear were folded in all the suitcases,
stolen motel towels lining the athletic bags. Time for a shoeshine;
no time for anything but good-byes, farewell drinks,

and motionless, transfixing waves. The branches were
whispering—or was it the leaves, heaped at the foot of
the wall?—but she whispered silently, along with them,
hummed without breathing a tune she remembered.

Please—accept no ambiguities, don't take "maybe" for an answer.
Take the longest woven cloth, tapestried perhaps with hieroglyphs
and pornographic representations of the saints, and drape
it around all his palaver, his unconscious snobbishness,

or take the most innocuous of those ethereal bouquets, wrapped in green paper, addressed with another woman's note, and proffer it to the newsboy; his trousers, rolled up to avoid his bicycle's chain, are the pantaloons of Spring.

BROWNSTONE, RUBBER HOSE

but the engine died   sunrose
    (talk to me)
three days' darkness

    no hope to turn
again   to a dark quay, castoff,
    castaway, driftwood & over-
turned—a bare footprint, salt-washed, Greek
on a planted oar

each letter overwritten tissue, writing slowed
halt & blind
    belated, unappeased   asking
        the blockage deriding passion
    flaccid virtue, gutless   uncontrolled
    carnal thoroughfare

I stalled & lied, forged amorous
    passports, threw them out unused
            (unusable?)

why is there no depth, why won't
    the expected fullness follow?
pressing foreseen
    ends, why don't they
take up their beds
    & walk?

& him, who's broken his own

   capricious mind, emptied out &
              filled it with Artaudian violence—
a way more surly, comforted
    than my own—

   a Memphis, embedded,
        pointless windings of unembroidered
   scholasticisms

 hours nothing but
    words, sifting &
 sifting us

      to where he moves
   back & forth
    only, dwindling
             (talk to me)

The Encroachment
Of History In October 1993

those times are
motionless, or when
you can't raise your shoulders
or head from the pillow,
when time makes itself
impotent or irrelevant—but two
rocket-propelled grenades
must have missed (barely, yesterday)
a helicopter over some
dust-baked country, some horn
of America—and trolling
the net proves us, not the
technological cowboys we had
(secretly) hoped, but the same
helpless arrested change—some-
one spreads his arms, letting
someone else's shoulders down
to laugh, but has your oppression
honestly outweighed mine? and who
keeps score?—Suffering, about that
Men like You and I are never wrong:
take that accident on the highway,
the overturned semi, the line of
battered cars, and the winner at
the head of it all, both blue ends
compacted, spreading glass
confetti, ambulances/firetrucks/po

licecars thrust up to him like sperm
to an egg, and the one non-
chalant hand dangling
out the driver's
window

Charles his ear

the pearl at Charles his ear, waiting for the storm
that refused to come   I used to tape
the windows of my ears against the shattering
now my waiting stand has dulled

the ridge over Jonson's nose brutal open mouth
a rushing burning moment when music seemed
to matter not just love, love, love a Covenant
he couldn't sign discipline he could not take upon him

    hypothesis:
the occult connections between Münster antinomianism
and Johnny Rotten Jean de Leyden Strafford's head
becomes an icon for the Thatcher State underwater linkages

that man—that preview, twenty-five years on—
couldn't be Cromwell, tearing down the high altar's
candlesticks—what Christian would do that?

alliance between the classical & the gutter
perfect form & locker-room jokes
the change will do you good open the till
money as the emblem of what drives poetry,
whose lines uncannily track the paths of currency

I once wanted to read *all* the books, as if that would validate
my eyesight hear all the records as a sea of sound
when your friend's adrift on a wash of cannabis

damaged goods the only linkages that matter
are electronic fund transferrals (or so I say)
that Parliament full of lunatics, men
of a single idea

no-one believes anything these days
send them back—just another council tenancy, which
nobody I knew understood at all *I don't
understand this bit at all*

   [*Anarchy for the U.K.*]

Milton's Empty

hard fire in Milton's empty
      eyes a world of tastes & smells
odors & breezes heats and
      colds the resplendent colors
of heaven translated to multi-
      farious taste & sound &
touch speak up for yourself
      or you won't be heard
beat them as stubble of the
      field mad unthinking
exultation as if one's enemies
      were God's as well Come
seare mee, seare mee, I shall beare
      in my body the markes of the
Lord Jesus Come friend, Come,
      burne mee, cut mee, I feare
it not. I have learn'd to feare
      the fire of Hell, and not what man
can doe unto mee: Bastwick's wife
      kissed his ears We are asked to
believe that a bee came and sucked
      honey from the flowers in his
hand My wife yesterday of her owne
      accord brought me these wedding
gloves, for this is my wedding
      day Shee is but a young
Souldier of Christ, but shee
      hath already endured many a sharp
brunt and cut him deep into the
      neck, neare jugular veine, to the

great danger of his life. the marks
 of the state engraved in the bodies
of the citizenry an antinomian
 tattoo beaten into cropped ears
so that he fainted from the pain
 of his tongue pierced pain
as option scarification as fashion
 adornment aristocracy engraved
in the aristocrat's pierced ears
 antinomianism in the
puritan's sawn stumps Jonson's
 branded thumb

[*Anarchy for the U.K.*]

COVNANT

        "nasty, brutish, and short"

they embraced each other, then parted
to their corners of the book
      that life among others is a state
of war is the state of nature
      the "state" of "nature"—whether
the Covnant stand with king or
      parlament, one is nonetheless
sworn thereto   they struck each other
      then parted to their corners
of the house

      [*Anarchy for the U.K.*]

LIVEFOREVER DAYGLOW

God coils himself in scales, painted glitter
ceiling a low cloud bank, and no respite

a beauty of wisdom and relation that destroys
a beauty that destroys motion, clarity, relation

he has compassed his face on the waters
fissured brazen Christ lifted on a dogwood

haloed his punctured head with St. Elmo's Fire
a ball of light body of glass hand of brevity

tender thy mercies o lord to me, tendentious
a crystal network binding the horizon

his beautiful thighs hard as missiles
sullen below, ground grey no motion

God snakes himself, coils, coins, currency
of architecture, speech, structure of emotion

Swimming

how can one stand it? to be walking down
the street, motion abstracted from malicious intent,

carefree as the day is long; that the compass
Urizen wields is rather a pair of pens

or a pointed graver, & his beard
"blowing over the abyss" an abstract spume:

when she said, you're unreadable, and when she
said, don't read me, and when he did anyway

so that the pages lining the walls were like
the blue crushed velvet between the twinkling stars

how can you stand it? she said, graver
than ever—*die Sau schwimmt,* and

Paul swims too

Broken Book

    suggest

    that
Christ was naked under
the robe, & that

when they seized
it, he fled
   naked

or the moment
    when the Angel
of the World strikes

between the lips
& nostril, wipes
    out

memory:

*

Contrails, foundling
brought faltering,

and only technology shows
the shrinking   of the periphery

*

> I take it
> this is nothing
>   but a game
> your words like
> a stripper at
>   the fireman's ball

[handwritten: Fluid, meaningless, is this the reader speaking?]

an oil, smoke black
the red bandanas
    tied at throat &
ankle   (or the black

leather
    stutter, churned coasting
& a pudding of piss &
                    mud

*

"tell it to Metatron,
        the lesser LORD,—he has written
    my troubles   out

of earshot, frost-
red eyes & silkening
glance

*

cold blue forest dreaming
   deep, dead &
dreaming white-skinned Jewish boys

stripped bare,   blue

veins to nipples
   purple fingernails"

STRUGGLE

      an open sonic
           space full only
of tension
        drums, opened
             bass, skittering
distortion of electric
        guitar

the struggle hand-to-hand, sword
to sword—beating down the enemy
as reaping the corn

beating the ploughshare into a sword,
the pruning-hook into a javelin

grotesque rhetoric of holy war
laser-guided ordnance, cruise
missiles the sword of the LORD's

angel over the threshing-floor
bruises splashed across the shoulder-
blades, hollow eye-sockets, protruding

cheek-bones—*anabasis, hejira,
exodos*—& you & I fight only with
words the meaning of their fight

let me ride on the Wall of Death I can't
get over the Wall the original "wall
of sound" let me take my chances on the Wall

> by the 1640s, the term *Puritan*
> can scarcely be spoken with straight
> face—Malvolio, Zeal-o-the-land
> Busy stage-Puritan stage-Irish

of Death David's census, as if numbering
were somehow not a crime, computation
an offence against the LORD

hegemony of angels, figures too emptied
out by a constant parade of imagery
    original frightening power

> *Note, also, how poem after poem, as disjunctive as it may seem, brings itself to neat closure with a quotation (real or manufactured), often in the witchery of semi-archaic diction.*

[*Anarchy for the U.K.*]

Cromwell's achievements

thinking in types comes
>   naturally the Hebrew
Bible tells story after story
>   for me to follow
for us to follow following us
>   Jesus iconoclasm in the Temple
of the heart no stone upon
>   stony Hebraic sweetness
patriarchs a sullen angry
>   grudge-holding & violent
tribe he tore down the candle
>   sticks like a blonde Jew
Sid's shoulders slick with the crowd's
>   gobs chest criss-crossed with
bottle slashes revolution as farce
>   my friend the Quaker Jewess
screaming across the stair
>   well Cromwell's achievements
(during the Protectorate)
>   readmission of the jews
to England I want to see
>   some history safety pin thru
the Queen's cheek nipple
>   pierced with heavy golden calf
Children of Israel slamming beneath
>   manufactured gods Baalim
and Peorim smash a thousand
>   Telecasters and Marshall amps

[*Anarchy for the U.K.*]

BASILIKON DORON

Basilikon Doron:
prohibiting dvells, witchcrafte
           sodomie

Noah's son uncovered his father's
           nakedness
in an act of buggery

Buckingham, Robert Carr, Esmé
           Stewart
the King's beloved dogges

St. Stephanos under a hail
           of rocks
Saul the coatboy

Sebastian swims on a wave
           of eros
Baby Steenie

      [Anarchy for the U.K.]

Eleven-odd propositions

1　　　There is no city, only shining suburbs.
2　　　The man's life is made out of words.
2.1　　The man's life, as seen, is made out of pictures.
3　　　The cigarette is essential.
3.1　　Robert Johnson, Louis Zukofsky.
4　　　There is no silence. Words happen in noise.
5　　　The trees move in the wind, but I can't identify them.
6　　　Big blue pickup truck, big white car.
6.1　　Sodding sprinklers wet my carseat.
6.11　 All faith is fanaticism. Q.E.D.
7　　　How many sonnets make an epic? Words happen in noise.
8　　　He's short, he's got ugly teeth, and he's wearing a bad suit.
8.1　　Eat each separate dish before going on to the next.
8.2　　Dogs in the midwinter, but the sun's beating down.
9　　　New Coke is Coke II in Lebanon. Words happen in noise.
10　　 Existence precedes essence, words are sequent to things
　　　　　　　　　　　　　　　　　　　　named, or vice-versa.
10.1　 Change the tape; you much change your music.
10.2　 In the sentence, 'if I were given the choice,' who's giving?
11　　 Words happen in noise; winds break down; maroon sports
　　　　　　　　　　　　　　　　　　　　utility vehicle.

The Effacement of Genitalia

scattered philosophemes
    demand equipoise
acumen scared enough
    to find that particular
entry, singular moment
    when the mind patterns
its rapacious peace—
    that the ploughs
in the fields, turning
    back and back again,
hit bedrock, marks scratched
    out and dug up, rubbed
over—lights of the library,
    across the broad dish
of turf, insects whirring
    around halogen street-lamps;
drought changes imperceptibly
    to rain—*Basilikon
Doron* to *Eikon Basilike*
    to *Eikonoklastes*, history
of England traced in
    the shift from full beard
to vandyke to clean-shaven
    Puritan—only a blunt
blade could give
    so close a shave, but
Petrarchan devotion lives
    only in the beloved's
absence; the models
    of "companionate love"

fall outside Laura's model—
    Damon & Pythias, H.D.
& Bryher, Duncan & Jess,
    Holmes & Watson, DJ
& JM, Eric & Rosalie—I've
    spent a week of hours
collating dates & places, a year
    of months rereading
poems, a month of sun-
    days... Jacobus R, "more
addicted to love males
    than females," nonetheless
"kissing her sufficiently
    to the middle of the
shoulders"—but what *I* want
    to know, the middle
dorsally or *ventrally?*
    essay on the efface-
ment of genitalia in 18th-
    century discourse: Gibbon,
e.g., surprized that his grapefruit-
    sized testicular swelling had
been noticed, blandly replies that
    he himself "never looked at other
people's *genitures*— "
    but "Be assured, my dear
Girl, that I have seen
    nobody in these rambles" and
"Do not live away from me.
    My Distress is great."
desire and learning twinned, cleaving
    together in the rind

of one fruit—attention rattling
    like a Vespa on a gravel
road, skidding in and
    out, at last
to some destination

Florida Poem 2

to move
        in the shine-dark
her palazzi and canals
        would use
more opening

•

traffic tied thru
        the next four exits
a darkened tollbooth
        below the salt
an afternoon rain

•

"his vocabulary
        hamstrung
tempered, but not
        unbroken—
warming the reed
        with an alien
tongue?"

•

mornings harder
       than late nights
daylight & artificial
       light, the thing
itself & its
       syllables

•

that story was too
       short, climbing
the brief hill to
       the railroad tracks,
beyond his father's
       garden

•

she started out
       listening for trains
over the hill, at
       the top
of the embankment—down
       the street

•

turn over—to the
      right—raise it
there, & stay
      still; I'll tell
you a story, but
      don't laugh

•

his mother covered
      the Volkswagen—
white—with stickers,
      beetles and flowers
on a cold day, it
      refused to start

•

crying out over
      the train-whistle,
her voice thru the warm
      airs, sounding over
dry grass
      and palmettoes

Pipe Bands in Alexandria

1)

One day you step through that door, the one
you're not supposed to open, and nothing
is the same afterwards.

2)

If he took to hiding things around
the house, how did that differ
from the other wee furry animals?

3)

So did the novelist love men or did
he not? Don't hedge, don't dance
around the answer—

4)

The train—for once—slows down,
pitch of the noise falling; one always
lives near the tracks.

5)

Ask the question again, slowly,
mean it this time. You want
me to answer?

6)

The darkness—by no means a tunnel
but a mist, a cloak—no, not
that romantic.

7)

No pure silence; beneath the insects,
always the distant whirr of the interstate;
silence dirtied noise.

8)

A phalanx of fiddlers on a blazing day—
sentimental tartans,
but the dogs never arrived.

wee song

      the Lord draws

no one

             picks its way
         across the bottom

                     the Lord draws no
                          one

   a tiny wee buke
      a broken gangrel

              flashing eyes

          stag
            hound

    take it
    like
        a man

turn again
home

            blackwater
              side

"the only food
she had

"never dance
again"

bread
& morphine"

strathspey

        sprinkled skirling
          words

voicelings

      lips parting
      under water

farewell
fareweel

                                          take back
                                          your name,
                                                your shiver

John—your
    pillow

                    Madonna of
                    the Rocks
                        footwash

                            Baptist

crystals on
    your sleeve

  auld black
   bitch of a
    boat

          neither coal
          nor candle

  scrape lichens
  from the stone—or
    "Charlie is my darlin'"

Couenant of Peace

"Have you forgotten the close,
      the milk house, the stable, the
barn, and the like, where God
      did visit your soul?" And
Phinehas, hee rose vp from amongst
      the Congregation, and tooke
a iauelin in his hand. 8. And he
      went after the man of Israel
into the tent, and thrust both of them
      thorow, the man of Israel, and the woman,
thorow her belly; ¶ And the Lord
      spake vnto Moses, saying,
Behold, I giue vnto him my Couenant
      of peace.

Is there not yet upon the spirits of men a strange itch? Nothing can satisfy them, unless they can put their fingers upon their brethren's consciences to pinch them there. Study to be innocent and it answer every occasion, roll yourself upon God which to do needs much grace. Know that uprightness will preserve you. I have lived the latter part of my age in the fire, in the midst of troubles.

                    words of the Lord and Lord
                    Protector translated

modernized punctuation orthography

                              itches of the heart (*leb*)
                              translated to words

the very Historicall trueth is, that vpon
        the importunate petitions of the Puritanes,
at his Maiesties comming to this Crowne,
        the Conference at Hampton Court
having bene appointed
                a most corrupted translation
        This much to satisfy our scrupulous brethren

The master is your creature, as the place,
And every good about him is your grace.
His pow'rs are stupid grown; for please you enter
Him, and his house, and search them to the center.

the time I shall never forget
        at Farnham, when the bed's head
could not be found between
        the master and his dog

A man with a good car
                needs no justification

        [*Anarchy for the U.K.*]

Circumstances Considered

the social text becomes the sexual, the henna-
    haired girl's pierced navel, tattooed arms &
        ankle, hardened nipples beneath cotton

shirt, tang of sweaty coiled armpit *by these Markes*
    yee shall knowe them—dominant culture/rebellious
        counter-culture, a model rocking on its con-
                              ceptual

feet: rather minority monied culture, borne artificially
    aloft on a thrashing sea of subcultures
        it seemed pretty natural (stark mad retro-

spectively) to take that primitive
    church as social model take seriously
        Jesus' injunctions

        I my self, have seen 17 or 18 Villages on Fire in a Day, and the People driven away from their Dwellings, like Herds of Cattle; the Men murthered, the Women stript; and, 7 or 800 of them together, after they have suffered all the Indignities and Abuses of the Soldiers, driven stark naked in the Winter through the great Towns...but, *I do say*, that Circumstances considered, this War was managed with as much Humanity on both sides as could be expected, especially also considering the Animosity of Parties.

the military text becomes the sexual, to covet victory means
to covet the vanquished's wives Brennus's
phallic sword thrown on the unequal

scales of defeat 21 And they vtterly destroyed all that was in
the city, both man and woman, yong and old, and
oxe, and
sheepe, and asse, with the edge of the sword.

he works, says J.H., in the old, modernist
mode, places, says C.R., block upon block,
hoping vainly they'll add up to a tower,
a wall, a broken cathedral

                          brittle music

                          of struggle, unheard

                          since that day

                          in Ithaca—today,

                          yesterday,

                          the bombs patiently

                          unwind their way

                          into buildings, homes

                          bridges, trucks

                          in electronic
                          silence

the thieves on their crosses: "two to one ratio
of collateral damage, Commander"

        [Anarchy for the U.K.]

HER PROPER VOICE

dig, he said, writing
an archaeology image of God
in works of men, time, weather
and always marks fragment
of speech or bit of paper
one would hear those voices *the earth
has stopped her tongue*

       I never knew her myself, but would sing
       that song gladly, retail the story ten
       or twelve times removed

*a glimpse of paradise / across a dull and bitter
       land*
her proper voice absent, blown away
in a swirl of ideologies, drowned
by a drum machine & sequencer a cloud
    of witnesses sheen of synthesizers
making memorable the voices of their enemies
by casting them in cadence of Scripture:

    —What thinkest thou of thy husband now, woman?
    —As much now as ever.
    —It were but justice to lay thee beside him.
    *—If ye were permitted, I doubt not but that your cruelty
would go that length; but how will ye make answer for this
morning's work?*
    *—To men I can be answerable, and as for God, I'll take
him into mine own hand.*

I am come, he said—according to one history—to set a man
at variance with his father, & the daughter
against her mother, and the daughter in law against
her mother in law

                in another murky Tiepolo, Jesus's eyes
wild as a broken-backed dog's.

I want to see, he said, some history!, the *r* trilled
    like a mad
Northumbrian's—"All that which you call history, and have
                                            doted
upon it, and made it your idol, is all to be seen and felt
within you"

    [*Anarchy for the U.K.*]

Video Memories

Eating ceding the initiative
    to word themselves, freckled
    and fabulously sunlike, bouncing
    artificial balls pushing unmotorized
          scooters across the four-laned
    street. Blackened grouper on a bed
    of mashed sweet potato, asparagus
foundation. The wind blows the mid-range
          away, leaves only the drums,
    bass, the cymbals—a purplish bruise
    on the beach's face, where flotillas
    of broken glass wash the bases
    of umbrellas, striped. White tie and vest
          pixie mistress ten years younger
than the greybeard's wrinkled asian eyes. Pick
    at the scallops with a fork, steamed
    clean in machinery, watching
          prosthetic girls go by—dark glasses
glow with moonlight. The new patented non-
    defective mnemotechnic, it works thru cash-register
    receipts, contracts, advertising flyers, credit card
    statements—Common Era of blockish
          numerals, simplified Arabic. *The number
of maidenheads*—said T—*are there any virgins?*—said
T—*where's the point of this*—said R—*and how
    did you get there?* the style, say I—or *stylus*—
    is—or makes—the point. *I'm so very happy*—
said J, awash in papers, trumpet mutes, slang,
women in drag, and binary codes—where two is one.

THE FACTORY

Who's to say the machine isn't running
rightly, cogs & wheels black with grease
or oiled like a head of lettuce?
The architecture of funds, progeny
of earthly happiness, felicity of spikes?
Landscape disappears in a flat country
of regnant, open sky—sunlight portioned
out in crown-sized slices. Vehicles' spaces
buffet one another at speeds cushioned
beyond sound, birds' latin recast
into Horace's or Tully's, whose chick-pea
name is lost only when the machine
falters, gears grind & slip. The University
produces, like a precision-spaced assembly
line, funds & Capital, money and money's
Mother—grinds its mills smaller or coarser.
Glaukopis Athena, eyes flashing like olive
leaves in a Caribbean wind, had an owl
as familiar. Silver rings & studs tattooers'
ink exfoliating bleaches hair dye & silicone.
Mousse gel & spray. Rinse & repeat.

Writing Ruskin

He sits down to write. On his desk
is a new biography, reviewed in the *TLS*,
the *New York Times*, the *New Yorker*.
He writes, addressing John Ruskin
in the second person, present tense:

>   *The last bridal taper burns down; you draw*
>   *the curtains of the bed, where she huddles*
>   *beneath an embroidered counterpane. "Euphemia,"*
>   *you breathe*

no, that's not right—

>   *"Effie,"*
>   *you breathe, almost a moan, and pull*
>   *back the coverlet. In the dim light, alabaster*
>   *flesh, two blushing almost marble breasts, long*
>   *curve of belly, and then, like an unexpected*
>   *rodent, the shocking triangle of hair*

—and so forth, from instant detumescence
to feverish denial to ultimate annullment,
hopeless, unrequited pedophilic yearning,
and decades of laying down the moral law
in purple prose. He jots down two final
quotes, to work in somewhere:

*"he had imagined women were quite
different from what he saw I was, and that
the reason he did not make me his Wife
was because he was disgusted with my
person..." "Though her face was beautiful,
her person was not formed to excite passion. On
the contrary, there were certain circumstances
in her person which completely checked it..."*

A baker's dozen of morals from which
to choose: 1) great men have feet of
clay, particularly when it comes to sex
2) passionate moralizing arises out of fleshly
frailty 3) innocent girl, bursting with young
life, rejected by pale aesthete 4) Patriarchal Hatred
of the Feminine Strikes Again! 5) Victorian
depilatory habits carefully considered—
He sheaths his pen, pushes back
his notebook. Enough material. This is
enough. Enough for now.

The Passing of Eeyore

The bear's hindquarters are stuck in a rabbit-hole.
Christopher Robin reads from a book.
He reads the word JAM.
"Jam," says Pooh, "I am jammed in this rabbit hole."
"Jam," says Christopher Robin, "is preserves.
In a jar."
"Jar," says Pooh, "perhaps jarring would free me."
The boy's hair is cut in a graceful pattern one sees
only rarely, on young women and small girls,
never little boys.
The bear is naked but, like Adam and Eve,
unaware.
"Desire," says Pooh, "grows out of others' possession."
"I do love you," says Christopher Robin, "silly old bear."
"I love you," says Pooh, "because you love
the others. If I were free of this hole,
I would tear the lot of them
to bloody ribbons. Piglet, Eeyore,
Kanga, Tigger, Roo."
A bear does not live, the encyclopedia says,
by honey alone.
"Silly old bear," says Christopher Robin, "if love
were a triangle, where on it would I fit
the six of you?"
Owl stoops from a pine-tree branch, seizes
and kills a field-mouse. He drags its body
in the dust, signs his name WOL.
"Silly old bear," says Christopher Robin, "how could
you tear them? You haven't any claws.
And stuffing has no blood."

Love the stuffing at a holiday dinner. Your wife
is Piglet. Your husband is Tigger. Roo, or Pooh,
is your child. Kanga is your nursemaid.
"Eeyore's house," says Pooh, "is no dream.
We moved it, inchoate bundle of sticks,
in a driving snowstorm."
The sticks float under the bridge.
Eeyore, blue plush waterlogged, fetches
up downstream.
"Silly old bear," says Christopher Robin, "be quiet
while I read." JAM. WOL.
"They dragged the river," says Pooh, "but found him
four miles down, two days later.
Plush too wet for burning."
Love, Christopher Robin reads, makes you real.

THE HOLY BEDE

                              (James, dreaming)

a thing of the past, my
        thirty pund knights, thing
of the past Buckingham's dog's-
        tongue licking at my
ear—Cherlie's gane tae Spain, awa,
        Cherlie's gane wi Babie
Steenie—stoned, stone-cold
        my ballocks.   the hair gray
around the royal sack

                    In to the swerd the cherchè keie
                    Is torned, and the holy bede
                    Into cursinge

        the church key turned—locking
                out or locking in? 1640, a drunken
        soldiery vent their fumes in breaking
                altar rails, breaking down
        the walls

broken doors windows cracked panes
        of stained glass martyrdoms
his body knotted down head between
        the knees fingernails pressed
                into the horny soles
        of his feet
voices about him of children singing
        a woman singing to the egg

     and seed coiled together in her belly
    Edmund Ludlow, *belly broken & bowels*
torn... hip-bone broken, all the shivers
     and the bullet lodged in it
     'o cousin, kiss me before I die'
(bearded lips to bearded lips)

        And ye shall cry out
        in that day
        because of the king
        which ye shall have chosen
        you and the Lord
        will not hear you
           in that day

'stumbling down the steps in darkness, the rail...
    wet with blood, blood
       on the steps'—and those blonde,
empty-headed twins buying liquor
      on sixth avenue, girls baring
    their breasts, marked with tattoos
       & rings of Baal & Ashteroth   plastic
      beads & plastic money paper
      promises plastic explosives

your skin so sweet   *your sweat so sour*

–hello, honey—wha'd'ye want to do with me tonight?
–*by God I have leapt over*
   a wall, by God I have
–ooh, isn't that naughty? now I'm lighting
   a cigarette—can you hear me?
–*through a troop, and by God I will*

>   *go through*
> —now I'm taking off my dress—can you hear me? your voice
>   is so soft, so sexy
> —*this death, and he will make it*
>   *easy to me*

>   What are all our histories and traditions
>   and actions in former times
>   but God manifesting Himself
>   that He hath shaken
>   and tumbled and
>   trampled upon
>   everything that
>   He hath not
>   planted?

[*Anarchy for the U.K.*]

TOURIST

      deny the charges, challenge
the court's jurisdiction
    (white-haired blood-boltered
hands knuckling the wheel)

        At home he feels like a tourist

        bodies sifted in sandy
        graves shallow marsh grasses
        swamped insect-buzzing
        flatlands bodies sifted
            nameless into lowland church-
            yards tangled among
            grassy roots

that faith should be the hand
    pressing them under, fist
breaking the saddle-bones
    numbering the bloated dead
        flocked over by ravens washed
up on beaches for the dogs
        to gnaw

        among the lost at Marston Moor, the white
        spaniel Boy, who leapt over men's
        and horses' bodies, who sniffed
        the trembling hearts of
        his master's enemies

Felton, the Kinge's Dogge's
> thin-lipped dagger the arrow
that searched out – finally –
> Steenie's life
> *there's many ways to get what you want*
All things are lawfull vnto mee, but all
> things are not expedient *I is the*
>> *best* Be not deceiued: neither fornicatours,
>> nor idolators, nor adulterers,
>> nor effeminate, nor abusers of them-
>>> selues
> with mankinde

And as a cunninge imbroderer havinge a peece of torne or fretted velvet for his ground, so contryveth and draweth his worke, that the fretted place being wroughte ouer with curious knottes or flowers, *Doe ye not see this poore Bee?*
> *She hath found out this very place*
>> *to suck sweetnesse from these Flowers;*
> *And cannot I suck sweetnesse*
>> *in this very place*
>>> *from Christ?* they farre excel in shew
the other whole partes of the velvet: So God being to worke vpon the grounde of our bodyes, by you so rente & dismembred, will cover the
> ruptures, breaches, &
>> woundes, which you have made, with
so vnspeakable glory, that the whole partes which you lefte shalbe highlye beautifyed
> by them

these sites, now greened- or constructed-
    over
the bodies – for the most part – anonymous,
    stripped by camp-followers and Egyptians
He fills himself with culture / He gives himself an ulcer

    'Sonne, Sonne, what is the matter
you look so pale?'

    [*Anarchy for the U.K.*]

FIRE & BRIMSTONE (Pillars of Lot's Wife)

Intense, white, a face fractured
into thousands of pixels, pressing
the story upon us again:

        the aged filth-bearded
        Avraham, dickering with
        the Nameless, fifty, forty-five,
        forty, thirty, twenty,
        ten...

Bally Prada Louis Vuitton
    Rolex Sony Visa
Nokia Microsoft Absolut
DKNY but a visour, or cloke, to hide
their Sodometrie withall: onlye spoken, not
prooved: forged in the deceiptfull Mint
of their owne braynes

        He raiseth vp the poore out of the dust
Giles Corey, who would plead
    neither innocent
        nor guilty, pressed (*not prooved*)
    to death in Massachusetts
lifteth vp the beggar from the dungill
        to set *them* among princes make them inherit
            the throne of glory

>   forty-three
>   years after
> the regicide, fire
>   & brimstone in his
>   tightened eyes
>   *It pleased the Lo: to call for me*
>   *sometime*—Roger Williams, home
>   from Narragansett—*and with some persons,*
>   *to practice the Hebrew, the Greek*
>   —he taught Milton Dutch—*Latine*
>   *French*

inextricable
            tangle of languages
bifurcate towers of Babel
            tangle of sodomies electronic
fiduciary incests goats & sheep
            divided again
& again
                        for the pillars of the world *are* the L<small>ORD</small>'s,
                        and hee hath set the world vpon them.

as if there were nothing more to say *you can't*
hear them narrow eyes extorting
                        complicity, monosyllables
                        flags & bunting
                        irruption of history
that sends the poets scrambling
for pen, pencil, word-
processor

>   Spellbound lizards dart into
> the underbrush, over the rocks. The fire
>   burns through that man's
> cheeks, smashes his spectacles
>   into his eyes.
>
>   [*Anarchy for the U.K.*]

Mark you

       he ran, & without stopping
twisted himself, falling
     into a knot, forehead
          to the cinder path, glasses
     knocked askew

Remember this: it was all a memory,
or dream. Mark you, how he falls without
sound. Volume muted. Pause.

     desert mountains gleaming
          city, proud towers
        polished with emerald, proud
flesh, fitted platinum
        words crawl across news-
     print fire-ants biting at one another
     hovelled anthill to hovelled
         anthill: Brother, Enemy!

Wisdom cries curtained in the street, a shout
in the street, down behind
     a hedgerow, & money moves
     on perfect lubricated
         fiber-optic rails cables
         of fabulous bandwidth
     pumps reconstituted data packets
         into the chilly air, bodied
     with bones & flesh, the legs
eyes & arms of money, cruise missiles

        with lions' faces bodies
        of men wings of locusts

This to remember, write it in a book,
bind and seal. And the taste thereof
was sweet.

                the L*ORD* *maketh the earth emptie*
                maketh it waste
                vpside downe   scattereth abroad
                as with the maid, so her mistresse
                as with the buyer, so with the seller
                as with the lender, so with the borower
                as with the taker of vsurie
                      vtterly emptied, vtterly spoiled

    a glaze of water on the weathered
    deck; a drowned world, the air clear
    as cut and fitted glass; blue of water,
    green of water, mild drumming
    of water in aluminum drains

The airplane's belly slides over dishes
    of distant water, sunlight flaring
from ponds, streams, deltas, the cold
    air flowing recycled, recirculated.
It is all a memory, a dream: remember
    this.

    [*Anarchy for the U.K.*]

ALBATROSS

He walked, it is said, on the water
a stone on the water, sank like a stone
      a source, after all, of arrested
      movement—the mists reaching out
      to embrace spars and ropes,
      bulkheads and decks—through the fog
      the horn, very word like a bell
the glittering eye the loud
      bassoon he stoppeth
      one of three

    getting rid of the albatross
        the white robe white
        bird, burden of
           the past

    still the spirit of sixty-eight
        scratching, nagging
           guitar whine, a bottom
        into which the whole sound
        might fall, warmth of bass
bearing up the high end *albatross*
        white of the eyes
           over the iris
        a steady, staring mad-
ness, calculated extremity

      I've seen you up far too close
      I know you very well
      you are unbearable

Richard Rumbold, guard at the scaffold where Charles
 bowed his comely head,
 Down, as upon a bed
—himself on the scaffold, 1685:

>*None comes into this world*
>*with a saddle upon his back, neither*
>*any booted and spurred*
>*to ride him*

  words for a t-shirt, traced white
  on black, traced misty grey fading
  into white

peace, be still

   [*Anarchy for the U.K.*]

Rote Song/Valentine

What's that on the rocks?
dark & rote, splash on
rime—take stock, time
stark & mock by rote,
mock sadness, time glad-
ness in rime, rock in
time by rote, mark
thyme & madness, stocked
rotation in love's gladness.

MARK SCROGGINS is the author of *Louis Zukofsky and the Poetry of Knowledge* and a forthcoming critical biography of Zukofsky. He has edited *Upper Limit Music: The Writing of Louis Zukofsky* and a selection of uncollected prose for *Prepositions+: The Collected Critical Essays of Louis Zukofsky*. He lives in South Florida with his wife and daughter.

S P U Y T E N   D U Y V I L

Day Book of a Virtual Poet   Robert Creeley
Track   Norman Finkelstein
Columns   Norman Finkelstein
A Flicker at the Edge of Things   Leonard Schwartz
The Long & Short of It   Stephen Ellis
Stubborn Grew   Henry Gould
Identity   Basil King
The Poet   Basil King
The Runaway Woods   Stephen Sartarelli
The Open Vault   Stephen Sartarelli
Cunning   Laura Moriarty
Mouth of Shadows: Two Plays   Charles Borkhuis
The Corybantes   Tod Thilleman
Detective Sentences   Barbara Henning
Are Not Our Lowing Heifers Sleeker Than Night-Swollen Mushrooms? Nada Gordon
Gentlemen in Turbans, Ladies in Cauls   John Gallaher
Spin Cycle   Chris Stroffolino
Watchfulness   Peter O'Leary
The Jazzer & The Loitering Lady   Gordon Osing
Apo/Calypso   Gordon Osing
In It What's in It   David Baratier
Transitory   Jane Augustine
The Flame Charts   Paul Oppenheimer
Transgender Organ Grinder   Julian Semilian
Answerable to None   Edward Foster
The Angelus Bell   Edward Foster
Psychological Corporations   Garrett Kalleberg
The Evil Queen   Benjamin Perez
Moving Still   Leonard Brink
Breathing Free   Vyt Bakaitis (ed.)
XL Poems   Julius Keleras

Miotte	Ruhrberg & Yau (eds.)
Knowledge	Michael Heller
Conviction's Net of Branches	Michael Heller
See What You Think	David Rosenberg
Dancing with a Tiger	Robert Friend
MS	Michael Magee
A Spy in Amnesia	Julian Semilian
The Farce	Carmen Firan
Diffidence	Jean Harris
Spiritland	Nava Renek
Acts of Levitation	Laynie Browne
ARC: Cleavage of Ghosts	Noam Mor
6/2/95	Donald Breckenridge
The Fairy Flag & Other Stories	Jim Savio
Don't Kill Anyone, I Love You	Gojmir Polajnar
Ted's Favorite Skirt	Lewis Warsh
Black Lace	Barbara Henning
Little Tales of Family & War	Martha King
Warp Spasm	Basil King
The Desire Notebooks	John High

Spuyten Duyvil Books are distributed to the trade by
Biblio Distribution
1-800-462-6420
www.bibliodistribution.com

tues
wed